Dark Child Awakens

By Peter James Hickman

Published by
The Hickman Initiative

Edited by
Susan Hickman

Copyright © 2021 v4
Peter James Hickman

Paperback ISBN 9781777662905
eBook ISBN 9781777662912

@pjhvan

DEDICATION

To all my family, especially my sister Mary and my son Andrew: Your support, your unconditional love and your participation in my life have meant more to me than you will ever understand. It has kept me going--has even kept me alive--during my darkest times you knew nothing about.

To my late Uncle Dawson and Aunt Margaret, thank you for being my family. More recently, I think of you as the parents I lost long ago. I value your love and friendship above all else.

To my sister Susan and my daughter Sarah: I miss you.

To my friends near and far, young and old, new and long-time; I thank each of you for the influence you have had on my life. I remember all of you well and most of you fondly.

ABOUT ME

I am a son, a nephew, a brother, a father, and an uncle.
I am gay.

I wrote these poems as therapy to help me deal with the emotions I felt late in life about my childhood, a childhood filled with love, anxiety, pain and betrayal.

They were written to help me understand my powerful feelings, the harsh words of one-time friends and the anguish I suffered coming out in my late 40's some 10 years after I realized I was gay.

I married young and had two children before I realized I was gay. How is that possible you ask? I ask it too, but it is so.

Mainly these poems and thoughts were born when I came out. They reflect my feelings at that time, my awakening, the struggle of seeking out and being in gay relationships and the search for love in the gay world.

This anthology was written between 1994 and 2021. Each is my own original work

Enjoy, Peter Hickman
February 2021

DARK CHILD AWAKENS

Dying father; Crying children
Hurting family; Denying parent
Shifting lives; Fading light

A child alone; Lost in time
Loveless home; Painful lives;
Crying aching hearts
Descending darkness

Childhood lost; Siblings split apart
Mother's love buried; Children suffering
Anguish; Darkness

Chaos rules; Confusion reigns
Relationships formed; Relationships destroyed
Love attempted; Lives created
Fears hidden; Children born
Darkness descends

Relationships ended; Children awakened
Lives renewed; Children reborn
Children reunited; Darkness fades

Love found; New relationships discovered
New ways explored; Light flickers

Dark child reborn; Explosive renewal
Pain affronts; Truth revealed
Pain abounds; Love found
Light shines

Children saved; Children's children united
Hearts again filled with joy
Dark child awakens

THE EDGE OF ETERNITY

I stood alone at the edge
Seeking love
Seeking a new beginning
Wondering.

I imagined you in my dreams
Our voices met in space
Our minds entwined
We fell in love.

We stand together at the edge
A new reality facing us
Our pasts behind us
The future binds us
The world spins about us
A rose blooms for us
Eternity lies ahead.

JOY

I alone
You alone
Meeting together
Cynicism and doubt rejected
Optimism and hope renewed
Shared philosophies
Whispered words of love
Hearts filled
Joy found within.

FRANK'NESS

Lost childhood
Facing pain
Optimism discovered
Lost
Wandering

Self-discovery
Maturity
Youth
Energetic lovers

Discreet
Hearts exploring
Dancing
Loving
Sensual
Renewal

An ending marriage
Children learning
A new beginning

Seeking a life lost
Changing desires
Imagining you
Vision shared
Love aroused
Life changing
Joy found

Future hope
Together at the edge

FLEETING GLIMPSE

As a child I caught a fleeting glimpse of youth
I turned to look but it was gone
I cannot remember it clearly now
The child has grown, old dreams are dead
New dreams exist now

WINDS OF LIFE

As the winds of my life blow in new directions
As the winds of your life meet mine
As the winds of our dreams entwine
Where will these winds take us?

As the threads of our lives unfold
Will we be together safe and warm in our new reality

Let the world spin outside our door
For you are the only one I want to see now
And when you are here in my heart,
I don't even hear the wind.

ETERNITY

I dreamed of being in love long before I met you
I dreamed of being loved long before you were here
We have so much to share
How enjoyable eternity will be.

I dreamed of love long before I found you,
I dreamed of being safe,
Now I have that too.

I dreamed of sharing my life,
I dreamed, not in despair.
I dreamed of love and now you are here,
How enjoyable eternity will be.

ACHING HEART

Life without you is unbearable,
Life without you is inconceivable,
What is my aching heart to do?
What is my loving soul to think?
You are the cure.

I DREAM OF YOU

I dream of a love worth dying for,
I dream of someone who loves me,
I dream of a life to share,
I dream of an eternity together,
I dream of you.

DISCOVER

Will we ever truly understand the love between us
The love that binds us?
What will become of us as we grow old together?
Will our love survive the ages?
Survive the reaches of time?
So many questions
Perhaps our lifetime together will reveal the answers

SHARING THE WALK

He who wants to share the walk with you towards
the sunset of life, wishes you a happy new beginning.

Knowing that you exist has challenged my cynicism
and renewed my optimism of what I began to doubt
two people could offer one another.

Seeing your face, feeling your heart and sharing the air
that you breath has
shown me a feature of life's face that I hadn't seen before.

Being with you has taught me a new dimension
of what sharing is really meant to be.

Whoever made you has definitely left a mark of himself in
you, and proven to me that he has made you to be the one
I thought could not exist.
I was wrong.

You make me feel safe,
You make me feel wanted,
You give me energy that cannot be consumed by work.
You give me hope for a lifetime
You give me life
You make me complete.

CONDITIONS

I dared to dream of someone once,
A person filled with unconditional love and wonder.
Of you

I expected not to find the person to be a mere mortal in reality.
It was a mystery when I found you,
How my dream could come true

Where does this wonder lead?
Where are the conditions?
Where is the doubt?
Where is the anxiety?
In my dream it was not there,
But in reality?
With you it's not here either.

Does this mean that unconditional caring
Is possible on such a scale?
Can two people discover the wonder of life together?
I can,
I have,
With you.

TE AMO

The first time however foggy is lost in the past
The first time it felt like the first, last and only time
The first time I never knew that it would be the
    beginning of what seems to have been there all along
I don't know why but I find it difficult to believe that this
    may not just be a love affair that will end when
    the sun goes down

I don't know why but I can't seem to remember
    when it all began
That first coffee we never had
The first time we looked into each other's eyes
The first time I ever saw eyes smile at me

So, what happens now?
Where are we going to?
I want to ask
I need to ask
I won't ask

Could it be because I don't see the end just as I can't
    seem to remember the beginning as a beginning?
As if you and I don't have a beginning and
    therefore, no end
I don't know I just don't know. Do I need to know?
I DO know that you fill me with peace
You make me feel air under my feet
You leave me confused.

Te amo

TEARS

We met discreetly in the dark days of winter.
Crisp, snow filled streets surrounded us
My warm smiling eyes greeted you
Our eyes locked, you took my breath
A spark ignited, a friendship began
What you doubted might it be possible?
What I thought I might never find: is it here?

Many questions and restrictions faced us
As we walked forward together
I concealed things that I longed to say
Scared to reveal what I felt, but I did
I'm afraid I'll frighten you away; You were frightened
We were frightened together
Afraid of what the future held or didn't

On an event filled day you confessed your inner
    feelings to me
You declared your love, you declared your passion
Our tears flowed; new tears were formed: our tears

Can we see the possibility of a new life together?
Making hopes and dreams out of pain scars fears?
Now we can go forward confidently knowing we will be here
for each other
What a special day

A special day that brings much joy to my heart
I find myself wondering about our life together
Where will the future lead?
What adventures will it hold?
What pain, what joy?

Will we ever truly understand the love between us the love
that binds us?
What will become of us as we grow old together?
Will our love survive the ages survive the reaches of time?
So many questions we will be able to answer together

So many questions on this special day
Perhaps during our lifetime together we will discover the
answers

INNOCENCE BETRAYED

Do I have the power
At this late hour of my life
To realize the dreams I once had
As an innocent young lad

Where might those dreams have led
"Had I only been free," I said
Would the life I missed have been better
Or disappointing yet

The childhood betrayal
I fight to no avail
Anger, alcohol, sex and drugs
Are easy answers to soothe the soul
But they serve no noble goal

Am I yet worthy of a better life
Free from pain, free from strife
Have I not suffered yet enough
What must I do to be more tough

I dream at night of what life could be
But in the morning the same I see
How can I change my future now
Wishing alone will not tell me how

I must leave the past behind me
I'm not going that way
I must look forward you see
To a better brighter day hopefully

EYES AND SMILES

Eyes meet eyes, smiles, hearts glow
We dare to touch unspoken connections begin

Your finger touches mine, our hands encircle
Our hearts entwine
I feel your heart expand beneath my hand
It's just a feeling but I know

We talk, we plan without saying a word
Our lives begin to entwine, yours and mine, as we walk together

Where are we going? We don't need to ask we know
We speak volumes to each other without saying a word

TOGETHER

I hear your voice on the wind
It shouts to me like magic
I reach out

A fleeting glimpse, a passing moment in time
Minds touch and connect
Eyes meet, hearts glow
We feel safe and wanted
Energy abounds
Hope renews
Together we are one

PRINCE

You are the brightness, the light in my life
You are the crisp morning air,
The bright daytime sun,
The warm night winds
You are my prince

STARS

I stare at the stars in my mind
My soul is sometimes blind
I cannot see the future clearly

Who is that soul in the mirror?
Who is that frightened little boy?
Will his mind explode?
Has he reached a crossroad in his life?
Which way should he go?

Have I found another soul? A mate?
Or is it a reflection of my own?

I reach out, I decide
I may just find my way
I know what I must do
It seems so frightening; so new

What will I become?
How will I live my life?

I touch someone, my soul isn't blind after all
The stars seem brighter now

PEACE

The day draws longer as I await your voice
I can't seem to hear you above the crowd
I panic
I scream
I run
Your voice pulls me back
I am at peace again

CAN I STOP TIME

Can I stop time so I may enjoy this moment longer?
Have I found a soul mate to share my life?
I have a need, a longing that perhaps you can cure
Knowing you will be there allows me to let the clock tick on

JANUARY FATE

The Great War had just begun
My Nana bravely carried on
To Mumbai she went across the sea
Determined to marry her beau, Sydney

The lived a life under the Raj
With servants and a boy who laughed
My uncle born so far away
I've never met him to this day
The next war took him far too soon
He died that tragic day in June

His father followed him to the deep
My Nana got so little sleep
Anxiety it was she well explained
She and Mom were all that remained

Off to the country to be safe
They joined her brother in a place
Far from the bombs that came each day
The relentless attacks from Germany

At war's end when peace broke out
They all did cheer and loudly shout
Life settled back as they rebuilt
A country crushed to the hilt

Mom met Dad and married soon
Then along came a son and sisters two
A normal life for we three
Until that fateful January
A crushing blow to all of us
Dad died that day and broke our hearts

SPIRIT HELPER

My spirit helper wandered off I know not why
I was sure of the past and hopeful for the future
Then the present came crashing in
Endless confusion, endless emotion

I doubted you, I doubted us, I wandered
All that I held dear I flaunted
All that we wanted nearly shattered
I disrespected you and disrespected myself

Now I see that you truly love me
I have renewed respect for myself
My love for YOU enriches ME but gives me
    no claim on you
I dream of making you happy but I can't promise that
    for it would be unrealistic to think I had such power

I write what I feel in my heart and can only hope that you
want to continue this adventure together as much as I do

I hope for no greater happiness than to be your partner on
the road ahead

You are my truth, you are my spirit guide
I am home now

PARTING

We fly away across the world in opposite directions,
Yet my heart is content, I am not torn by emotional dread,
Why does my heart feel this way, I hardly know you,
Yet I trust that we'll be together soon.

I have found in you a happiness I had begun to doubt possible,
A chance encounter never planned,
Has shown me a new dimension of what two people can share.

It's different this time,
Bright smiles sparkling, eyes locking together,
Spice and water mixing
It is difficult to imagine this is just another trifling affair
This feels so real.

Meeting friends, parents, former lovers,
Each a confident statement of what we can have together.

Voices reach out across the void,
Hearts fill with joy,
Knowing we are here for each other.

MEETING AGAIN FOR THE FIRST TIME

We fly across the world racing towards each other
Hearts expand reaching out across the miles
My mind races thinking about our future together
What does the future hold? How will our lives unfold?
Tonight, we will meet again, never having left each other

SUNDAY MORNING

I love every minute that I'm with you
I love you every minute that we're apart
For as long as I know you are the one, I'll cherish every beat of your heart

FIGHT

I hate you
No, I don't, but I hate what you did
Your words made me feel less than I am

AWAY AGAIN

A single day away seems like forever
I awake as you begin your flight across the ocean to an
    island in the early morning mist
Lifting up and away from me, I imagine you working,
    helping, enjoying being you

I breakfast alone, yet not alone, knowing you are here
    in spirit
I enjoy, no, I savour the moment thinking of you
    far away
Knowing I will see you tomorrow, knowing you will
    call today

Your time away gives us space, space that binds us
    ever closer
You can't wait to call and I can't wait to hear your voice

I am at peace

COMMITMENT

The time has flown I hardly know you
Yet I know you well enough to know you are the *One*
Only *Eight* weeks, not even *Three* months or years
Our time together seems to have no beginning
And therefore, no end?

When I am alone now, I am content missing you
But feeling you ever present in my heart

No one else has ever made me feel the way you do
The way you hold me
The way you look into my eyes
The way you make me smile
The way you flatter me

I am never alone now, but miss your presence when you are not here

My commitment to you is real, true and sincere
I love to be with you
I love being a part of your life
I love it when you let me share your fears
I love it when you are less independent
I love it when you let me in
I love it when you laugh
I love it when you cry

You will never be alone, for I am here for you in every way

Our commitment to each other is obvious
We are both in the right place space and time
We both have needs that the other fulfils
We are both happier now that we have each other

DID YOU EVER?

Did you ever love a guy and think he didn't care?
Did you ever feel like crying but knew you'd get nowhere?

Did you ever look into his heart and wish that
   you were there?
Did you ever look into his eyes and say a little prayer?

Did you ever see him dancing when the lights were
   turned down low?
Did you ever whisper "I LOVE YOU" and think
   he didn't know?

Did you ever wonder where he was at night
   and wonder if he's true?
One night you could be happy and next you
   could be blue

You see things might not turn out right between
   you and I
And if I had the choice of life or death,
   I think I'd rather die

So never fall in love again for you'll be hurt before you're through

You see, I ought to know I fell in love with you

EMPOWERED

At peace now
Love certain
Living life
Growing together
Creating new life
Planning the future
Excitement
Energy renewed
Healthy
Wiser
Relationship empowered

My spirit yearns for you always
Not knowing why

I am sure of my past and of the future I want with you.
The present crashes in
A whirl of endless change
Endless confusion
Endless emotion

You were my truth
Now I am my own spirit guide

CONTENT

Cry of the Gull
Horn of Yacht
Squeal of Tires
Tourist Bus
Laughter of Child
Strains of Music
Aromas of Dinner

Clouds passing
Surf breaking
Sails being set against the breeze
Freighters anchored, patiently waiting

Touch of a new friend
Beat of a new heart
Feels like home

I am content here

FALL AGAIN

Crashing Wind
Wild Waves
Buffeted Sailboats
Slashing Rain
People: braced as they crawl along the water's edge
Fall Again

KIND HEART, TROUBLED MIND

Today was much like any other
The sun and sky are there
I think, I breathe, I smile, it is a good day

Most friends are far, family too
I feel alone sometimes even though I'm not

History is a poor teacher, I a poor learner
Peace of mind seems fleeting, yet a noble goal

In my mind I travel through a tumble of life events
I love life, I love the vibrancy and variety of it
It energizes me, it fills my heart
I care so much it hurts, I love so much I fear
I will miss it so,

Kind Heart, Troubled Mind, Peace at Last

RANDOM

A balmy late August afternoon, warm sun
We met at random. A hook up; nothing more
It blossomed quickly

I was NOT looking for a new boyfriend
I had barely left the last
I was fixated on recovering from the pain
   and anger stored,
From being trapped in a relationship gone
   so badly wrong.

I was not open to anything but sweet afternoon delight
I did not want the responsibility that commitment becomes
It became so much more. I was surprised, thrilled ... wary

51% HUMAN, 49% UNDECIDED

My lids flutter. My eyes roll back.
I drift off. Sleep envelops me.

I stumble awake to his touch, aroused
His touch erotic, even loving.
Darkness embraces me yet again.
I sleep soundly through a lazy, hot,
Humid New York afternoon.

I stir as he enters the room, awake, rested.
He leans against the door frame.
How are you? he asks.

51% human, 49% undecided, I quip

TURNING 50   (For Tom)

Facing the year ahead with a new sense of worth and ease
Out of the blue you are struck with a potentially fatal disease.
Let me go, you cry, I do not need more pain,
I have had enough suffering. I don't need more again.

Ignore him, I whisper to the doc,
He gets like this when he's in shock
Start the treatment, we'll get through it
Family and friends, we'll all see to it.

LYING AT THE EDGE

Lying at the edge of sleep
The moon floats above unseen

Lying at the edge of sleep
Dreams break through the fog
Or are they memories, or Nightmares
Or a new hidden reality.

Lying at the edge of sleep
Dawn breaks. A fresh world awakes
Full of enthusiasm, dripping with opportunity.

It's Saturday!

FRAGMENTS

Shattered fragments reflect to create a picture all too clear
Decisions considered, ideas pondered, nothing to fear.

The eagle strums the sky as he reaches for the sun
Wind billows the sail as it steers away towards the distant horizon.

Wheels spin, blades roll, feet pound
the seawall comes to life
A new day unfolds

CABBAGES AND SEALING WAX

The table's laid, the plates arranged
The dishes filled with Pain
Bowls of anguish, suffering and regret, all so plain.

Let the feasting begin ...
The guests gorge themselves on all the tasty bits
The leavings cast aside for those less fortunate

"The time has come," I said aloud, "To talk of many things:"
The beginning is as always, the best place to start
That's the place that plays right to the core of my heart.

The naive JOY of it all. Innocence shattered
The troubled minds created that will take a lifetime to heal
The kind hearts that prevail passing on bounty to others.

INTROSPECTION

A Childhood remembered but lost in death
A Youth of torture, feelings suppressed

Adulthood abandoned to career and confusion
A Sudden awakening ends the illusion

My soul reborn, a sense of renewal
Joy found for a time before life turned cruel.

The future beckons, my fate unknown
Where'd I leave my blarney stone?

Likely next to my rose-coloured glasses.

MARCO

He sizzled up the driveway
Leaving the hot July day cooler in his wake
I looked down at my feet as to make sure they were firmly planted against the shockwave of his approach

A Hello I didn't hear?
A stirring I long thought dead.
I felt weak kneed, I felt lust
I was smitten by this man I did not know.

He left me to melt in his aura without knowing me.
Did he not know his own power or was he arrogant and aware of his heat?
I thought not.

Did I sense a bond that perhaps time would turn into something more or
Was that wishful thinking?
Was he forever beyond my reach?

WINTER STORM

The branches reach out like bony fingers to scratch
    the cold threatening sky

The evergreens stand guard against the approaching storm
The sky reaches down to touch the ground
The rain screams across the strait and into the city
    driving against the window like a sheet of silver
    shimmering in the darkness
The wind whips across the water smashing the whitecaps
into a creamy froth
    and it howls like a terrified wolf

The city is plunged into darkness
We are bundled up against the dark night fearless together
I feel you pressed up hard against me
I smile at the pleasure of your touch
My heart races at the pleasure of being with you

I love West Coast winter storms

I SOLDIER ON

Childhood vanishes
Voyage begins
Darkness enfolds me
I soldier on

I build a life
Chaos follows
I seek solace, even peace
I soldier on

Now mountains guard me
The sun warms me
The fresh sea breeze cools me
I soldier on

I laugh. I love. I live.

Armoured against the fray
The slate grey sky descends
Depression beckons
I soldier on.

Freedom rushes at me
Sickness scratches at my door
I soldier on.

I laugh. I love. I live.

Old Friends flee
New friends found
Old friendships renewed
Family gathers
I soldier on

Death leaves a mark
I soldier on.

SHADOWS ON THE SKY   (for Andrew & Sarah)

My path has been as elusive as a shadow on the sky
More of the sameness crushes me
I fear it

To risk is to try to thrive
To fail is to have succeeded at trying
To risk nothing is to do nothing

I won't let failure stop me
I will start again and again and again

For trying is a celebration of life
The measure of success is how we cope with disappointment
The only real failure is the failure to try

Like drawing shadows on the sky

SUNDAY AFTERNOON @ PJ's

I spy you from the safety of my perch against the rail
I feel the heat of your approach; you leave a cheerful trail

I smirk at your evil grin, at your obvious intent
You press against me, I feel your excitement

Single you ask? As if you really care
Lust is what you feel, I return your hungry stare
What are we thinking? This will lead us where?
Does that really matter? Do either of us care?

No, it's Sunday and afternoon lust is on the menu
Shall we go to your place or choose mine as the venue

Will we speak at all or simply dive right in?
Although we enjoy each other dressed
We crave the touch of skin.

Sweet Sunday afternoon Lust

UMBRELLA

The raindrops beat relentlessly on the once yellow umbrella
    that stands abandoned on the beach.
Firmly planted into the sand it braces itself against the
    watery onslaught hopefully out of reach.

A fishing boat staggers by drunkenly, making its way back to port as the steel grey sky swoops down to touch the sea obliterating the horizon from my view.

The red and green buoy lights flash ceaselessly ensuring its safe passage into the harbour.

I walk hurriedly but silently along the seawall, bracing myself against the driving rain but enjoying the fresh exhilarating sea air.

I pull my collar higher against the blustering wind.

THE INEVITABLE STORM

People say you only have one life to live.
People are wrong about that as they are about most things.

Dawn was still a few hours away.
I enter the room.
Is the life I am leading the same one I was living an hour ago? Two years ago?

I climb quietly, sleepily into bed.
I reach out, "I love you" I whisper.
"I love you too" he replies.
We embrace and tumble into frenzied love making.

A storm approaches.
It is still over the horizon, but there is lightening in the air.
Neither of us is aware of the lightening.
We are aware only of the electricity we generate ourselves.

Our first awareness of the storm is not the crash of thunder but rather the jangle of the phone.
Angrily he answers. There is only silence, then a dial tone, but he knows.
He tries to resume the love making, but his mind is elsewhere now.
I also know that nothing I can say will help reduce the turmoil in his brain.

We both lay in silence hand in hand
Awaiting the inevitable dawn, the inevitable storm.

SHADOWS & PAIN

I lay quietly in the dark
My mind reeling with ideas and fears
Staring out at the night sky, watching, waiting
Until at last the shadows flee before the breaking dawn

Another day beckons me.

The constant ebb and flow of the tide hides my sorrow
The brilliant sunshine gives me hope

Another day beckons me.

RAINY NIGHT

I hear the harrowing screams of rain drops pushed aside by the ever-advancing tires in the traffic below

I hear the throaty satisfaction from the drain swallowing the effluent sourced from the thundering rain

I hear the drum beat of disparate drops crashing against the glass, fleeing the balcony above, slapping incessantly on the rail

I hear the whispering of my past haunting my soul deep into the night.

Rainy Night in the city.

ALONE IN MY ROOM

Alone in my room
Safe from the virus
Alone in my room
Not making a fuss

Alone in my room
Locked up for days
Alone in my room
Time slipping away

Alone in my room
For too many days
Alone in my room
Free me from this cage

Alone in my room
Work just not safe
Alone in my room
Eating too much cake

Alone in my room
Thinking of family
Alone in my room
Netflix binging spree

Alone in my room
Watching the news
Alone in my room
Can't find my shoes

Alone in my room
Thinking of friends
Alone in my room
When will it end?

MENTAL DAZE

Some days I am defeated
Some days I function well
Some days I'm filled with anguish
Some days an empty shell
Just trying to survive

Some days I'm in a labyrinth,
Some days I'm just confused
Some days it's such a struggle
Some days I feel abused
Just believing I can thrive

Some days I feel truly broken
Some days I feel much pain
Some days I'm very hopeful
Some days there's joy again
Just glad to be alive

SINNER OR SAINT

Are you sinner or saint
It's all in how you paint ... your path
How you colour ... your journey

Are you saint or sinner
Just a beginner, or wise beyond years
Having dealt with those fears

Or are you a survivor
A legacy of your own path
Coloured your own way ... by your own journey

A JUMBLE OF DARK & LIGHT

Once I went out walking on a dark & windy day
I came upon a bench and rested on the way
Up above I saw an eagle climb the ragged sky
The lightning flashed; the thunder roared as people hurried by

I wandered deep into the night
Quite sure of what was wrong or right
My life a jumble of dark & light
The truth, the lies, the endless flight

A life lived in the shadows of something I can never change
No matter how hard I rearrange
I struggle on with all my might

Against the inevitable storm

I DON'T DO NORMAL

A normal life once long ago
Mom, Dad & sisters two
School & friends, fun I know
Then one day it went askew

The world broke apart for we three
We were each other's sanctuary
Packed up and off across the sea
Our lives were changed relentlessly

The pain still claws my back each day
Not strong enough to turn around
It finds me in the strangest way
Will likely chase me to the ground

Can you miss a life you never had
Do you wonder? Are you sad?
It's really a life you only feign
Long ago, branded by pain

Living in a shadow I can never change
So much time trying to rearrange
Each phase of life has left its scar
Some deep, some long, but never far

Restless nights I toss about
Memories crashing, always doubt
Can anything set things right
I wonder deep into the night
I wish I wish with all my might
Then comes the early morning light

Still fearful, trapped and alone,
Exhausted, hurt, even confused
Struggling to survive;
But no longer abused

LOST | FOUND | HOPE

I will not bow down to bullying
I will not bow down to homophobia,
    xenophobia, misogyny or racism.
I will not bow down to war or greed
    or words in old books.
I will not bow down to despair,
For me there is always hope.
And when you are near to being lost
You are equally close to being found.

That's what I believe

www.ingramcontent.com/pod-product-compliance
Lightning Source LLC
Chambersburg PA
CBHW062205100526
44589CB00014B/1958